Shrike Shrublands

Steve Jones

Published by Steve Jones, 2023.

SHRIKE SHRUBLANDS

First edition. June 26, 2023.

Copyright © 2023 Steve Jones.

ISBN: 979-8223199496

Written by Steve Jones.

Also by Steve Jones

Shrike Shrublands
Wildlife Watching Around Ventnor, Isle of Wight
Writers in the Wild

Watch for more at Stevecjones.uk.

Table of Contents

Dedicated to all those promoting natural regeneration as the best way to create new woodlands and open grassy-shrubland habitats! With your efforts, we may see the recovery of our Turtle Dove, Nightingale, Whinchat and Dormouse populations and, perhaps, the return of the Butcher Bird, to the British countryside.

If you enjoy reading this guide please consider leaving a review on your online bookshop of choice. This helps other people find it. Thank you.

1 Introduction

'Scrub' is a much-maligned habitat in official UK conservation and farming circles. Scrub 'invades' other habitats. Volunteers conduct 'scrub bashing' weekends. Farmers can lose public payments if there's 'too much' scrub in their pasture.

Of course, the colonisation of important old grasslands by shrubs and trees can be enormously damaging to their existing values if left unchecked. But very often valuable areas of scrub are removed without good cause. I recently observed as a local Wildlife Trust systematically removed small, scattered patches of Dogwood, Wayfaring Tree and Elder from otherwise very open chalk grassland on the orders of the statutory conservation agency, removing long-standing features and reducing habitat heterogeneity to no good effect.

Grassland-shrub mosaics can be enormously valuable, dynamic habitats. Yet we seem to resent their very existence and miss numerous opportunities to create more of them. A baffling example of this: many of our most prominent, respected, and influential nature conservation organisations choose to bypass the early successional stage of grassland-with-scattered-shrubs-and-trees in woodland creation projects. They instal solid plantations of even-aged whips (nursery transplants of trees and shrubs), bypassing the wonderfully biodiverse grassland-shrub mosaic stage of ecological succession that, under nature-guided circumstances, would be a normal part of woodland community assembly. I'm not suggesting that such dense planting isn't appropriate in some circumstances. I've done some myself. What I *am* suggesting is that extensive planting should not be the *default approach* to woodland creation where significant nature conservation gain is the objective.

The gradual, sequential, unpredictable colonisation of open areas by trees, shrubs and herbaceous plants is a fascinating and enormously important part of nature recovery. The natural process of species assembly itself is an attribute of biodiversity that should be valued.

In woodland creation projects, rather than planting wall-to-wall thickets of even-age whips, we should always consider aiming early on for a *mosaic* of species-rich scrub and locally disturbed, structurally complex, species-rich grassland with enormous value for wildlife, including many species of conservation concern.

As these grassland-shrubland mosaics develop they can give additional positive benefits: they can gradually absorb atmospheric carbon; attenuate rainfall and reduce water run-off owing to their roughness and gluey organic matter build-up; provide wonderful spreading space for people; provide high-quality, healthy grazing and browsing habitat for livestock and space for the conservation of rare livestock breeds; and, of course, be a cost-effective precursor to natural woodland and wood pasture development.

It's time we ditched the derogatory 'scrub' label and championed species-rich grassy 'shrublands'.

This short booklet seeks to encourage the creation of new species-rich grassland-shrubland mosaics - 'Shrike Shrublands' - **on existing species-poor sites**, such as hitherto intensively managed pasture and arable land, and amenity grassland.

The words 'scrub' and 'scrubland' are here replaced by the words 'shrub' and 'shrubland' to signify a more positive stance. I hope the term 'grassy shrubland' creates an image for you of a mosaic of grassland with scattered shrubs, rather than a thicket of shrubs. The latter is valuable but here we include the ever-so-vital flowering grassland element.

Why '*Shrike*' Shrubland? A couple of years ago I was asked to investigate prospects for the return of the Red-backed Shrike to southern England. During that investigation for the RSPB and the Knepp Estate in Sussex, I came across a 2002 paper by Dr Andy Evans and Des Vanhinsbergh (*Habitat associations of the Red-backed Shrike (Lanius collurio) in Carinthia, Austria*). In one part of that and a related paper the authors set out how one might create perfect habitat for Red-backed Shrikes. What was immediately clear was that perfect Red-backed Shrike habitat is one that contains a rich community of species associated with dynamic, open, often early successional habitats, and some of those characteristic species are of conservation concern here in the UK and across north-west Europe.

Their paper and my visits to the Knepp Estate inspired this booklet.

The Red-backed Shrike - the Butcher Bird - was once a widespread species across our countryside but is now effectively extinct in the UK as part of our summer breeding avifauna.

After their demise as a regular breeding species here, and a protracted decline in north-west Europe, prospects for a return to the UK of the Butcher Bird have seemed remote. But with very recent hints of recovery on the near-continent in response to habitat creation by farmers and a couple of favourable summers, we might just entice Red-backed Shrikes back if we create lots of favourable habitat for them.

So, if we can create new Shrike Shrublands scattered across the UK, we might just see the return of the Butcher Bird.

The perfect territory for a Shrike is good for such an enormous variety of species that creating this habitat should be enthusiastically encouraged regardless. This is truly a straightforward and 'no regrets' investment and the creation of Shrike Shrublands should be a central pillar of nature recovery across farmland.

This short book aims to advocate for this habitat and to give an overview of how to go about creating it.

1.1 Why do we need Shrike Shrublands?

The Red-backed Shrike is a wonderful ambassador species for a neglected habitat - open, sunny, species-rich grassland-shrubland mosaics.

Breeding Red-backed Shrikes have a specific set of requirements from a high-quality territory. If we can create blocks of habitat, each capable of satisfying a few pairs of nesting Red-backed Shrikes, we can be sure that it will be bustling with wildlife, including some other priority species of conservation concern.

1.2 What makes a high-quality Shrike Shrubland?

To paint a picture of the perfect Shrike Shrubland, let's describe the perfect Red-backed Shrike territory, then scale up so the shrubland can support a few pairs of Shrikes. Bigness is beautiful.

A high-quality Shrike Shrubland is comprised of *widely spaced* clumps of native, often thorny, shrubs - Field and Dog Rose, Bramble, Hawthorn, Blackthorn, Elder, Crab Apple - with the occasional taller shrub and emergent tree, distributed across a mosaic of very short-grazed lawns with scattered patches of disturbed ground, and areas of taller, flower-rich grassland.

Crucially, *large* invertebrates - beetles, bumblebees, grasshoppers and crickets, and dragonflies - are abundant. Larger members of those insect groups are among the main prey items of Red-backed Shrikes, including their broods and fledgelings.

An extensive thicket of shrubs lacking open ground is generally much less valuable and would be largely avoided by shrikes.

The Red-backed Shrike is a sit-and-scan hunter. They love to perch out on the strands of shrubs in open grassland, waiting for potential prey to come into view.

The hunting shrike really loves an unimpeded view. The thin strand of a Field Rose branch extending up above a small mound of bramble is the perfect vantage point, as is a fence post within or strand of wire crossing open, species-rich grassland.

It's mostly looking for beetles scurrying across the ground and bumblebees visiting herbaceous wildflowers. As soon as it sees a large invertebrate it flies quickly towards it and catches it, either on the ground if it's a beetle or grasshopper, or in the air if it's a flower-visiting bumblebee or hunting dragonfly.

It will then fly back to its perch or another one nearby to devour its prey. It will often skewer prey on a favoured barb or spine. Or, if there's a nest nearby, it'll take the food straight to the nest to provision its brood.

Shrikes have an inordinate fondness for larger beetles. They capture these on the ground. Favourite beetles include those associated with animal dung. Beetles using cattle dung seem to be particularly popular. There would have been plenty of dung when Bison and Aurochs herds roamed wild European shrublands. The dung of domestic livestock once supported these dung associated invertebrates too, but the prophylactic use of anti-parasitic Avermectin drugs has had a dramatic, deleterious impact on invertebrates shrikes depend on to raise their broods, so it's essential that such chemicals aren't present in the dung of animals grazing Shrike Shrublands.

Shrikes want their food to be easily accessible. For beetles captured on the ground, this means they want to be able to scan across nearby lawns of tightly grazed sward and areas of churned up ground. So tightly grazed lawns directly below and around isolated clumps of shrubs, say Bramble, Dog and Field Rose, and Hawthorne, are ideal.

But the beetles are scurrying between tussocky grassland or piles of dung, or, for some species, animal carcasses. So, for both the beetles and the Shrikes, we need an intricate mosaic of lawns and taller, rougher grassland with a bit of very light summer grazing, to provide the dung.

The bumblebees, also crucial for Shrikes feeding their offspring, need copious quantities of nectar-rich wildflowers from early spring throughout the summer into late autumn. Both the shorter lawns and the areas of taller, more tussocky grassland should thus be a mass of flowering herbaceous plants from early spring to late autumn.

Bumblebees and other nectar seeking invertebrates love sheltered, sunny swards. The microclimates created by an intricately varied landform and scattered stands of shrubs are perfect. Streams and clean water pools within and close to the shrubland will draw in dragonflies and damselflies.

That's the basic ingredients of a good Red-backed Shrike territory. Now scale up and imagine a patch of that habitat capable of supporting a few territories side-by-side. That's a Shrike Shrubland.

Although the Red-backed Shrike is essentially extinct as a regular breeding species in the UK, climatic conditions for it are widely suitable here and are projected to become more favourable for them through time due to anthropogenic climate change.

But Red-backed Shrikes will not track their climate space unless they're doing well on the near-continent and habitat is available here in the UK. If their populations on the near continent increase, and they come to saturate habitat there, migrant shrikes may increasingly spill into the UK each spring. Creating Shrike Shrublands along the lines outlined in this short book will do a lot to welcome shrikes should they be in a position to attempt to recolonise.

But providing this habitat is about much more than just providing a welcoming habitat for any shrikes seeking to establish territories. It's about creating blocks of habitat that will support an array of wildlife.

Some key elements of a wildflower-rich shrubland

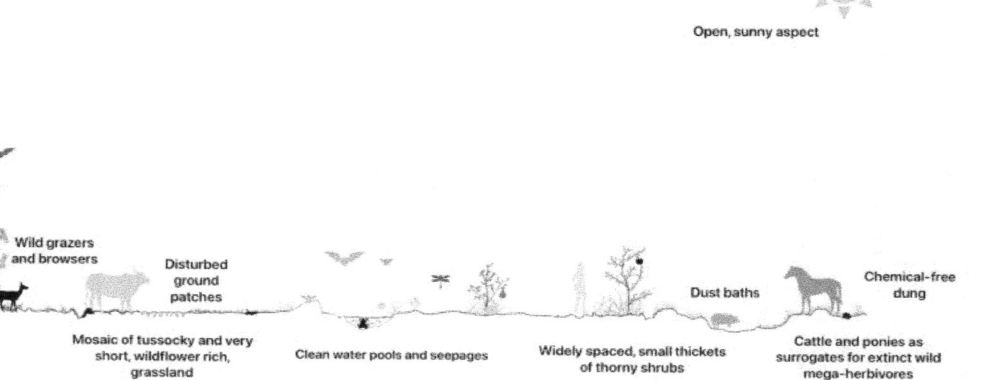

1.3 Biodiversity values

A shrubland-grassland mosaic with the various attributes outlined in this guide will be capable of supporting a high abundance of plants and animals and a richness of species. In the early years it will likely support many species characteristic of early successional habitat. Over time, species associated with older habitat features will likely appear. If the site initially lacks old trees with rot holes, for example, species associated with such micro-habitats will only start to appear after many decades. Greater complexity needs time to develop.

In this section, I'll very briefly highlight a few species that may well come to use created, open Shrike Shrublands in the early years. For a thorough deep dive, read the free JNCC report, *The Nature Conservation Value of Scrub*, a copy of which can be found via the link provided at the end of this booklet.

First, a shrubland of the sort described here will support many flowering herbaceous wildflower species. This community will be dominated by hitherto commonplace wildflowers that once graced most or all farmed grasslands. Species present within a given site will vary depending on conditions at a very small scale: tall areas of grassland will contain some species not present in more tightly grazed lawns; wet flushes will support wetland loving species; dry, summer parched areas will support species adapted to drought. Disturbed ground will support yet a different set of species. This kind of complexity of conditions brings with it diversity and richness.

A richness of flowering species will ensure there's nectar and pollen available from very early spring through summer and into the late autumn. Some wildflowers will even bloom through the winter. These need not be rare species. Just a rich assemblage of common wildflowers.

An extended flowering season is vital to the lives of many dependent invertebrates. Different species of bumblebee for example have different flight periods during the year. Whatever the species, and whenever they're on the wing, they need lots of wildflowers to provide nectar for fuel.

Abundant flowering species helps support rich invertebrate communities. Again, these will be overwhelmingly common and widespread species. Many of them will have declined greatly in abundance in recent decades. Because there's a mosaic of both taller grassland, and very short grazed lawns, bumblebees will find abundant nest building opportunities. Common grasshoppers will also be very much at home in this intricate mosaic of sward heights and structures.

Animal dung will be a frequent and ever-present resource scattered widely. Because this is free of toxic anti-parasitic chemicals, it will provide vital food resources for various invertebrates, including beetles favoured by shrikes.

The edges of scattered shrub mounds will likely provide sheltered basking spots for reptiles such as Common Lizard and Adder. Bush crickets will thrive here too.

Common bats of various species will find plenty of food over a Shrike Shrubland. Some scarcer species may utilise the site if they're in the area.

Several notable birds of conservation concern may well breed within Shrike Shrublands depending on their location, context and habitats within and around them. Turtle Doves, for example, may nest within thicker shrub patches, especially if there are clean water pools and annual seed-rich habitat within the shrubland or close by. Shrublands positioned within mixed, wildlife friendly farmland with arable is probably best for them, if the arable includes spring cereals and areas of fallow through the summer. Linnets are also an obligate seed-eater and will be present year-round. They tend to nest in small colonies within pockets of shrubs distributed across open grassland. Patches of Bramble and Gorse embedded within a grassy shrubland will more than likely support a colony of Linnets.

Nightingales may well colonise, but their tastes are not yet fully understood. They're to some extent a species of early successional habitats, perhaps where they're somewhat moist rather than summer parched.

Open shrubby habitat of this nature supports Dormouse on the Isle of Wight and in parts of Dorset. Hedgehogs will probably much appreciate a shrubland if they are present in the area.

Cirl Buntings are currently restricted to the south-west of England. But the population has increased dramatically over the last two decades due to concerted conservation efforts. They may well expand along the south coast east into Dorset and Hampshire. A Shrike Shrubland is likely to come into its own as a grasshopper-rich summer nesting habitat for Cirl Buntings if there's sufficient annual seed-rich habitat nearby support them over winter. Although the all-important disturbed soil patches within a Shrike Shrubland will support broadleaved annual wildflowers, a source of seeds needed by Cirl Buntings through the winter, these alone will probably not be enough to see the buntings through the late winter and early spring 'hungry gap' when weed seeds have been depleted by hungry beaks and invertebrates are scarce.

Blocks of Shrike Shrublands, as well as hedgerow systems, interspersed within arable with some spring cereal cropping are likely to be needed to support Cirl Buntings (and Turtle Doves).

Yellowhammers seem to range more widely than Cirl Bunting and remain widespread if no longer common. This is the most likely bunting to utilise Shrike Shrublands for nesting in summer in regions with mixed farming.

If your site is close to or contains within it wetlands, dragonflies and damselflies will likely be common. In late summer and autumn hunting dragonflies can be especially abundant in this kind of habitat.

It's important to note that the account above addresses the early years of a shrubland. Those sorts of results and values will persist if your shrubland is managed in the long-term to maintain an open grassland-shrub mosaic. But if your longer-term aim is to develop woodland, there will be a fascinating and natural turnover of species, with open habitat specialists tending to be replaced by those of cooler, more shady woodland habitats, including an array of scarce species. This will take many decades to unfold.

1.4 Woodland creation as an unmet opportunity

Native woodland creation is a high priority in the UK, and this priority offers an exciting route to create a shifting mosaic of Shrike Shrublands across whole landscapes and regions. To meet this opportunity, Shrike Shrubland creation could come to largely replace the common practice of wall-to-wall planting of nursery tree and shrub transplants (whips). Dense planting of whips usually rapidly bypasses open, sunny, early successional mosaics of seedling trees, shrubs and grassland advocated in this booklet.

Dense planting is partly designed to address often high mortality rates of whips. But it also leads very rapidly to a continuous, low, closed thicket across the whole planted area. This is entirely unsuitable for nesting Red-backed Shrikes and many of the other species associated with its habitat.

In the context of new native woodland creation, Shrike Shrublands can be a temporary phase in the gradual development of closed canopy woodland or more open wood pasture.

If most, or at least many, current native woodland creation projects opted for assisted natural regeneration, to plant trees and shrubs as *scattered clumps* in open grassland or on arable, rather than for extensive planting of wall-to-wall whips, we would see a shifting mosaic of open Shrike Shrublands initiated across our countryside. As advocated here, efforts would be made to enhance the wildflower richness and density within the open grassland component, too, recognising that this will ultimately be replaced by species favouring more shady conditions.

Numerous new grassland-shrublands could be created annually; we'd have every successional stage represented numerous times and ever-changing wildlife communities associated with each.

Where the long-term intention at a particular site is to retain a more open flowering grassland with scattered small thickets of shrubs, appropriate management can be used to maintain a more permanent, but dynamic, open habitat.

1.5 High nature value farming or rewilding?

Anyone can create a Shrike Shrubland. Not so long ago species-rich grasslands with scattered shrub clumps, as well as wood pasture, were characteristic of our farmed landscapes. Shrubland-grassland mosaics would certainly fit in very well with regenerative and other forms of high nature value farming and provide excellent space for rare livestock breeds, many of which are mixed feeders (enjoying both shrubs and herbaceous vegetation.)

Although the British Isles were extensively wooded, more open mosaics of species-rich grassland and scattered shrubs and trees were also a natural, pre-agricultural feature of the British countryside, just the sort of habitat likely loved by Aurochs and Bison across large parts of Europe. So the creation of Shrike Shrublands can also be an example of active rewilding.

Shrike Shrubland creation is for everyone. Every farmer and landowner across the country, whether they consider themselves to be a high nature value farmer, a rewilder, or a bit of both can create this wonderful habitat.

1.6 Long-term development

Suppose you have a plot of, say, five acres you'd like to turn into a Shrike Shrubland. In your mind's eye, how do you expect your shrubland to look in 20, 50, 100 years' time? Are you looking to stand back and just allow it to develop under its own steam? Are you specifically looking to create an area of high-quality natural woodland? Perhaps you envisage wood pasture, with grazing livestock or wild herbivores, or both. Or perhaps you'd like to maintain an open, dynamic mosaic of shrubs and grassland for the long-term?

Your choices will determine how to treat the site in the decades to come, but a Shrike Shrubland can and should be a prelude to all those trajectories. We'll consider your longer-term aspirations at points in the following two sections, addressing shrubland creation, and long-term management.

2. Creating Shrike Shrublands

In this section of the guide we'll first discuss some generic components that are likely to be present within most or all high-quality Shrike Shrublands. We'll then briefly outline how one might integrate these various generic components within three stylised contexts: arable reversion, open improved grassland, and woodland edge.

2.1 Selecting a site

Size and shape: This booklet deals with larger blocks of habitat rather than linear hedgerows with margins. The latter, without doubt, can be enormously valuable for wildlife within farmland. Hedgerows and flower-rich margins distributed within high nature value farmland, with, for example, species-rich grasslands and low-intensity arable, will be very important for wildlife.

There is a good collection of books setting out how to manage linear hedgerows, field margins and similar features.

Here, we deal with larger, round or rectangular blocks of habitat.

By larger blocks, we mean areas of several acres or hectares to tens or even hundreds of acres or hectares. The larger the better. If you have, say, a five acre arable field or paddock, that would make a superb shrubland for a pair or two of shrikes. As the size of the area in question increases, so too does its biodiversity potential.

Bigger sites have more deep interior, less influenced by what's going on at the immediate margins, and can support larger, and perhaps denser, populations of various species. They can also embrace a broader range of conditions such as soil moisture gradients and topography, boosting species richness.

If you intend to allow cattle to graze your shrubland, and this is certainly recommended if the dung is free of antiparasitic chemicals, then embedding the site within a much larger grazing unit could work very well. Hemming any livestock into a relatively small site, especially in summer, will substantially reduce its value. If cattle can range across a much larger area and only visit the Shrike Shrubland every few days, say, or as just occasional animals, this will help to ensure flowering plants can bloom abundantly and that a mosaic of herbaceous vegetation will be maintained throughout the summer.

Consider wild fire risk: In their early stages of development, areas of open grassland and scattered shrubs can be vulnerable to wildfire. In time, they may become less vulnerable.

Some attributes of the habitat described below may reduce fire risk. For example, reinstating seepages and creating networks of pools can provide effective breaks to grass fires. Lawns of tightly grazed sward and disturbed ground breaking up more tussocky grassland can also be effective firebreaks. Avoiding very large blocks of shrubs can also limit the extent of any fire damage. It may be wise to consult your local fire service if the intended shrubland sits adjacent to potentially vulnerable properties or infrastructure, including railway lines and highways.

Existing biodiversity value: It's important to audit the biodiversity value of your site before you consider creating a Shrike Shrubland. You should aim to pick a site with limited existing wildlife value. If your site is already designated, or recognised, for its existing wildlife value, it may well not be a suitable site to create a Shrike Shrubland. If legally designated for wildlife, consult your local statutory nature conservation agency.

If locally recognised as being of value for wildlife, consult your
County Wildlife Trust.

22

2.2 Starting land use

The current use and history of the plot of land you're planning to turn into a shrubland will influence short-term interventions, on-going management, and long-term habitat development. Let's look briefly at existing uses.

Existing Grassland: does the site have existing botanical value? Is it species-rich grassland? If the site is agricultural grassland that has been intensively managed in the past, it's unlikely to have much value. If the site is amenity grassland within a town or village, the situation can be less predictable. It may have escaped artificial fertilisers, and although regular mowing would prevent flowering plants from blooming, they may still be present in the sward. Some urban amenity grasslands are very old and very rich. Not just grasses and wildflowers, but also scarce lichens and mosses. Are there open-habitat species such as Curlew or Lapwing? Are there notable invertebrates associated with, say, open, sunny seepages?

Arable: arable fields often support the last surviving remnant populations of once widespread annual plants ('arable weeds'). These may not be obvious if they're holding on in the seed bank. They may reveal themselves if an arable field is allowed to 'tumble down' as fallow in the early months of shrubland creation. If the site in question supports populations of rarer annual wildflowers, it will probably be best managing it as low input cereals or cultivated fallow. More widespread annual wildflowers can be accommodated within disturbed areas that are integral to Shrike Shrublands

Forestry: many plantation forests were established at a time when the countryside was still of extremely high wildlife value, before agricultural intensification really set in. As such, many plantations were inevitably established on areas of existing wildlife value. Because soil and landform disturbance were often fairly modest, such sites may well retain both the landform and some of the wildlife of the habitats they were established on. Habitats include ancient woodland, heathland and species-rich grassland.

Forestry plantations often offer unusually good opportunities for woodland or open habitat restoration.

Brownfield: If the site was previously developed it could well have considerable existing biodiversity value, and it would be wise to consult your local Wildlife Trust, Biological Records Centre and national organisations Buglife and the Bumblebee Conservation Trust. Some nationally important invertebrate sites are long-abandoned, previously developed 'waste ground'. The site may already be known to be of value; or it may not have been visited but has all the ingredients of a good invertebrate site.

Archaeology: Surface or sub-surface archaeological remains could receive added protection (if, for example, arable land is reverted to grassland), but could also be damaged (if a clump of shrubs is established on such remains, or if sub-surface drainage is 'broken out' across such remains). Seeking the advice of a County Council or local university archaeologist may be wise.

2.3 Some early interventions

Below, we'll consider some early steps you might take to set your site up. You'll find a menu of interventions, some or all of which might be appropriate for you. Your aim is to set the site up in a way that provides a template for diverse plant and animal communities to develop.

This may require no initial work at all - just stand back and enjoy as species recolonisation under their own steam. But if the site has been improved for agriculture, or used fairly intensively, some early interventions can greatly improve how nature re-assembles itself.

Below, I highlight a few measures you should consider.

Reducing nutrient levels: Very fertile soil is the last thing rich communities of grasses and wildflowers need. You really need to take action to reduce nutrient levels as far as possible if they are elevated to an extent by past land-use.

If the land is arable, and soil sampling indicates that it is very fertile, unfertilised arable crops could be sown in the spring and harvested in autumn, with a stubble left over winter, and a further spring crop sown and harvested the following year. Do not fertilise crops at all: the idea is that the crops will soak up nutrients from the soil. These are, effectively, sacrificial crops whose sole purpose is to consume soil nutrients as much as possible.

If you're dealing with existing agricultural pasture, one option would be to close the site up for the summer, and harvest a hay crop in mid-July, when the grass is still green. Remove all the hay cuttings. Harvesting when the grass is still green will help to export nutrients away from the site. It would probably be beneficial to take several hay crops each year, one in, say, May, as long as ground nesting birds such as Skylark and Meadow Pipit aren't present, another in late July. Repeating this process over two or three years can only improve the results in the long-term. Remember, the richest diversity of grasses and wildflowers are found on infertile, not fertile, soils. Fertile soils simply favour the most nutrient hungry species, and these are few in number and very aggressive, outcompeting everything else.

Delay any other intervention until this has been completed.

Re-wetting: The countryside, even what one might at first glance consider to be 'dry land', well away from streams and rivers, more than likely contained wet features - flushes and seepages - that were removed as part of the agricultural improvement process. I cannot stress enough just how common such features once were, and how much inadvertent damage has been done by their removal.

If the site has been under-drained, one should consider making efforts to reverse the effects of that drainage. In-field under-drainage should be blocked or removed entirely. Side drains at field edges should be dammed using soil and/or woody debris. If there is sufficient tree cover around the site, and streams within and around it, it goes without saying that you should seriously consider including Beaver re-introduction within your project.

Why attempt to reinstate lost seepages? Because small-scale and seasonal moisture heterogeneity - wet spots interspersed amongst drier spots - can be key to supporting the varied life stage requirements of many invertebrates. Moisture heterogeneity will in turn support plant species diversity. And birds like Snipe will often visit wetter patches within otherwise dry fields on passage and in winter to feed.

Patches of moisture, especially if they are fed by springs into the summer, can persist even in droughts. Plants such as Meadowsweet and Ragged Robin may well appear within the sward in such damp spots.

Micro-landform: Landform at a tiny scale is usually extremely varied within natural habitats. This varied micro-topography is the template upon which so much diversity of species and communities develops.

If your site has been used for farming, often some of these intricate landforms will have been removed. Arable farmland will have been cleared initially, its surface levelled to some extent, with on-going ploughing further simplifying small-scale landform.

If the site is currently grassland, it may well have been ploughed, under-drained and re-seeded. And bulldozers may have been used in the distant past to remove infield hollows and hillocks.

If, on the other hand, your site is previously developed brownfield, a variety of landforms could already be present. Equally, if the site is covered in plantation forestry, relictual landform may well have survived.

More varied microtopography will result in a more intricate mosaic of habitats.

How can one put back a varied micro-topography? Initially, mechanically!

Ultimately, wild animals will create their own variety too.

Don't forget to consult your local County Archaeologist as appropriate before doing any land-forming. You might even need planning permission, in which case check with the local development control team in your council.

Use diggers to shallowly scrap off and pile up topsoil, creating sunny banks of friable soil. The bare exposed subsoil will provide the perfect substrate for the development of drought-loving plant and animal communities. Fertile soil is the enemy of high-quality shrublands. The sunny side of low banks will be colonised by whole communities of burrowing invertebrates.

Dig hollows of varied depth and extent. Some will be wet over winter into spring and then dry out, potentially being colonised by interesting wetland annual plants.

Others will hopefully hold water over the summer. Scattered clean-water pools - temporary or permanent - are a crucial element of the best Shrike Shrublands.

Mark out scattered cultivated plots: Mark-out areas you intend to cultivate if cultivated plots are to be part of your shrubland. Leave these areas free from other interventions because you'll be cultivating them every few years.

Scattered areas of disturbed ground are an enormously valuable habitat. Historically, Wild Boar would have been a key ecosystem engineer, creating disturbed plots via their rootling behaviour. Extinct wild cattle and wild horses would also have created forms of disturbance, but these would have been qualitatively different.

Wild Boar is very much a neglected native species in UK conservation. Hopefully, we will develop a recovery plan for this species. In the meantime, it's likely to be absent from your site.

It might be appropriate to include domesticated pigs as a short-term substitute for Wild Boar.

Creating brash piles to encourage Rabbits (see below) will introduce a degree of disturbance of great value.

Otherwise, marking out areas that will be cultivated infrequently can act as a substitute.

Plots of a metre or two up to about 10 m² would be ideal. The size of these plots will partly depend on the size of your site. Lots of widely scattered smaller plots are probably more valuable than one or two much larger plots.

Have quite a few amounting to, say, 10% of the site. This is a guess.

Aim to cultivate each plot on a varied timescale. Cultivate some annually, others every three or four years, some every five to eight years. Again, this is really guesswork. You're just trying to create a varied longevity of disturbance. This promotes varied successional stages, each of which will support different wildlife.

I'll leave this by restating that Wild Boar would do exactly this job much better than we can. So, getting them back is, ultimately, essential.

Create brash piles: Brash piles are an excellent hack for Shrike Shrubland creators.

If you're faced with a very open grassland or arable site, creating widely scattered piles of brash can really speed-up the nature recovery process.

A brash pile can be comprised both brash and larger logs. They serve several purposes.

Although Rabbits aren't a native species, they are recognised as a valuable 'ecosystem engineer'. The small pockets of disturbance they create provide shifting opportunities for annual wildflowers to maintain a foothold. Many invertebrates need annual wildflowers, and many need disturbed ground. Rabbits also create the grazed lawns - short turf patches - where Red-backed Shrikes love to capture beetles.

Rabbits drawn to brash piles often initiate new warrens within them, creating small loci of disturbed ground and shorts swards surrounding a brash pile on which a shrike can site and scan.

Brash piles can also attract Song Thrushes, Blackbirds and other dispersers of seed, enabling tree and shrub colonisation and germination.

Reptiles, such as Adders, will frequently bask next to piles of brash and find refuge within them when disturbed.

Dead vegetation, including dead wood from larger branches and logs, support a rich array of wildlife.

Plant introductions to overcome dispersal limitation: Excuse the rather geeky terminology: what this essentially means is that many plants face constraints on their ability both to reach a site and to establish themselves if and once they arrive.

Dispersal and establishment limitation are the main reasons why so many woodland creation projects rely on tree planting (although planting on these grounds often isn't justified, and other, less convincing justifications for tree planting are often invoked!)

The capacity of plants to appear at your site partly depends on its history of use, its current land cover (e.g., bare arable versus thick agricultural sward), its proximity to populations of plants, seed and seedling predation rates, and the presence, or absence, of means of dispersal (e.g., seed-dispersing animals).

Below, I first consider trees and shrubs, after which I'll consider herbaceous grasses and wildflowers.

Introducing islands of shrubs: densely planting whips of trees and shrubs across the whole site will *not* create the kind of habitat that is the focus of this book. Although such planting has its place, I urge you not to do this if you're aiming to create species-rich grassland shrubland mosaics in the early years.

Planting *widely dispersed groups* of trees and shrubs is, though, a valuable intervention to address both dispersal limitation and establishment limitation. It is also a good way of speeding up the process of shrubland development.

Foresters worry about high mortality rates of planted whips, and so justify dense whip planting as a way of mitigating that problem. People aiming to create Shrike Shrublands either as a permanent, open habitat, or as a habitat that will go on to develop as woodland or wood pasture, need not concern themselves too much with moderate mortality rates, if everything dies, you'll need to replant of course. A very common cause of such a failure is that the route mass is exposed to the wind just before planting. Ensure roots are kept moist and away from drying breeze and sunlight and water in copiously during planting.

If your site is directly adjacent to a patch of native woodland, you probably don't need to plant anything. Similarly, if it's surrounded by hedgerows with both trees and shrubs, allowing natural colonisation should be the preferred approach.

If you plan to plant, you should aim to establish widely scattered islands of mixed shrubs and trees species. Plant small nursery transplants (whips) rather than larger specimens. These tend to have higher success rates than older, standard trees. That said, there is something to be said for planting one or two Crab Apple standards within a site. This species provides two excellent keystone resources - blossom and fruits - much appreciated by invertebrates, birds, and mammals.

The species planted will depend on site characteristics, the region you're in, and the composition of local tree and shrub communities. There is plenty of guidance online, and your local Wildlife Trust should be well placed to offer suggestions. The Woodland Trust produces decent guidelines on this too. On the off-chance that Red-backed Shrike does recolonise, include shrubs that they favour. That includes Field and Dog Rose, Hawthorn, Blackthorn, Crab Apple, Bramble etc.

If your site has or is visited by wild or domestic grazers and browsers, you should consider protecting planted trees and shrubs. Rather than encasing each whip within a plastic tube, consider creating fenced exclosures. These are designed to exclude larger grazers and browsers. They are temporary and can be removed once the planted whips have formed an island thicket.

How far apart should your clumps of planted trees and shrubs be? This partly depends on what your long-term objective is. But I suggest spacing each clump of trees and shrubs every, say, 10 to 15 m. Don't plant each clump as a regular grid: vary the spacing.

You can afford to plant whips close together within these clumps. It would be well worth trimming whips down to ensure there is a reasonable balance between root mass and twig mass. This helps establishment.

Introducing herbaceous flowering plants: Basically, we need to get lots of flowering plants established in our open areas of grassland as quickly as possible. A wildflower-poor grassland-shrubland mosaic will be of limited value.

It can take decades for appreciable populations of flowering plants to colonise a site naturally. That slow pace is fair enough if we have time to kill and are relaxed about the rate of nature recovery. In my opinion, we should avoid importing purchased seed and attempt to source material as close to the site as possible. We are really only now discovering local adaptations in plant communities.

But nature is so depleted by us that really we need to intervene to speed up its recovery. And some barriers to colonisation of your site will be entirely human imposed and probably insurmountable for many species.

The invertebrates that need a variety of flowering plants throughout the year for their survival cannot wait a few decades for them to appear. Higher trophic levels of animals will begin to assemble if diverse and rich flowering plant communities are present. Invertebrate biomass will, generally speaking, be increased by diverse flowering plant communities.

Some sites may have wildflowers already present on site or around its edges. These at least have some chance of colonising and expanding within the site. But the presence - or rapid development - of a thick sward of grasses can present a formidable barrier to flowering plant colonisation.

Sourcing wildflower seed to plant. Whether you're starting with grassland or arable, you'll need to find a donor site or sites that support the species of wildflower you want to see within your shrubland. You'll be collecting green hay and seeds from this donor site in late summer. The closer it is to your shrubland creation site, the better.

Try to match the donor site conditions to the receiving site conditions. If your shrubland creation site is on chalk, find a nearby donor site that's chalk grassland, for example.

You need to make sure you don't harm the donor site. If it's an SSSI, you MUST consult the statutory nature conservation agency (e.g., Natural England) as well as the landowner. If it's a County Wildlife Site, consult your local Wildlife Trust. If you're unsure, consult both as a precaution.

You'll probably want to talk to the Wildlife Trust to identify potential donor sites and their owners in the first place.

Only harvest seed from a given donor site or part of the site once in three years. This helps to avoid any harm from over-harvesting.

Harvesting donor hay/seed. The key here is to harvest hay/seed at the donor site just as seed is being set. If the volume of material needed is large, a tractor-mounted forage harvester is best. A strimmer can be used to cut a smaller volume of hay. Apparently, if the hay is slightly moist this can help seed to stick to it. But don't leave your cut hay in piles for any length of time. Get material from the donor to receiving site as quickly as possible. Piles of cut hay can heat up rapidly, potentially damaging seed and reducing germination rates. Plantlife recommends that the operation of cutting, transport and spreading of donor material be completed within half a day.

Sowing/spreading. You need to break up the sward. Ideally, you'll have created cultivated plots within the wider grassland. These plots, which are additional to those to be cultivated every few years, will be the focus for creating areas that are species-rich in wildflowers, from which they can subsequently spread more widely across the site. Spread the hay very thinly, avoiding piles.

To ensure seed has contact with bare soil, roll or stamp it in, or put cattle on. Their hooves will push hay and seed into the soil surface.

Growing and planting wildflower plugs. You should consider growing on seedlings of a few common flowering species to then plant out into established grassland. This can be an effective way of getting over establishment constraints. It complements spreading green hay onto disturbed areas. It's more time-consuming but can be highly effective. You might even involve local schools in collecting seed and growing them on.

Immediate aftercare: The key here is to ensure that germinating seeds and planted plugs aren't immediately overwhelmed by existing, potentially more competitive grasses. If you've sown seed or spread hay into small, scattered patches, you might strim and rake off to keep the sward very short and open. You can also put on cattle or ponies in the early autumn to graze off the sward. Avoid significant poaching.

Arable is an easier starting point. Bare arable land provides a bare template without the competitive grasses that can prevent wildflowers establishing themselves in improved grass swards.

If the arable soil is rich of Phosphates and Nitrates, probably the best initial step is to sow unfertilised spring cereals for a couple of seasons. These hungry crops will deplete the nutrients at least. Phosphate removal is far harder and probably not worth even trying. It will gradually deplete over decades or longer.

Stripping away excess nutrients using arable cropping will set the soil up for wildflower establishment.

Once your arable site is ready, you can deploy the techniques already described in combination to inoculate it with wildflowers.

Don't bother with a commercial wildflower seed mix! These are extremely expensive and unnecessary.

As with the grassland example already discussed above, spread green hay in relatively small patches rather than across the whole site.

Management of an arable site during the year following initial establishment: The year after green hay has been spread, germinated wildflowers will establish themselves but, being perennials, few will flower. They'll do so each spring and summer thereafter.

If the soil is more productive and sward starting to grow on in that first late winter/spring, put on a few cattle or ponies to reduce the biomass. This will reduce competition and help the wildflowers get established. Shut-up the site by remove stock from April to July for the first summer or two.

Afforested sites: In parts of Europe, Red-backed Shrike numbers have increased within plantation forestry clearfells relative to wider farmland. The last few pairs of this species were found on afforested and more open heathlands on sites in the Suffolk Sandlings and the New Forest. More recently, nesting attempts have taken place on lower upland shrubby heath sites on Dartmoor and elsewhere. It's not clear whether such habitat is favoured by the species, or simply represents suboptimal habitat that nonetheless has been less intensively managed than the wider farmed countryside and so held on to shrikes a bit longer. I suspect the latter. Recent successful breeding attempts on

Dartmoor may simply indicate how hostile the wider countryside has become.

If your site is a non-native pine plantation, you can usually simply leave it following harvesting. Quite often such sites are on poor, sandy soils and the ground surface hasn't been seriously altered prior to planting. It may well contain a buried seed-bank of typical acid grassland, heathland or chalk-heath species.

3 Three stylised examples

Having described some of the components of a high-quality Shrike Shrubland and the kind of interventions you might consider in creating one, I'll now give three contextual examples.

The first involves an arable reversion site on a few hectares or acres of lowland chalk. The aim in this example is to create a long-lasting, open Shrike Shrubland.

The second example is a block of improved pasture. It's probably been drained and re-seeded in the past and received regular inputs of nitrogen fertiliser. Again, we're aiming to maintain open shrubland in the longer term.

The third example is on neutral soils next to an existing Oak woodland, where the aim is to expand the woodland and, in the early years, entice some specialist dappled sun loving butterflies to expand into the early successional habitat from coppice and rides maintained for them in the woodland itself.

3.1 Arable field on chalk

Let's assume for this chalk arable example that the site is very open, free-draining and sunny, and the intention is to maintain an open shrubby grassland mosaic in the long term through conservation management.

You're aiming ultimately to create grassland that is both rich in flowering plants characteristic of old chalk grassland, and therefore pollen and nectar, but also more structurally complex than is often the case with open chalk grassland. So, you want taller areas of grassland, tussocks, interspersed with more tightly grazed flowering lawns, and areas of bare recently disturbed ground.

Unevenly distributed within that open, flower-rich grassland will be small pockets of shrubs and a few larger, thicker areas of shrubs, with scattered tall shrubs and trees in some of those clumps.

Context: Paradoxically, a site where there's no existing vegetation, such as an arable field, probably represents the easiest starting point for the creation of a Shrike Shrubland.

The bare ground of arable provides a clean slate for colonisation, with fewer constraints. Whereas an established sward of grasses represents a difficult place for wildflowers to colonise, with lots of competition from grasses and few spots in which new seedlings can germinate, bare ground is largely free of competition and that's just what many seedlings need. You need to make the most of this situation quickly, because some highly competitive species can rapidly colonise and outcompete the herbaceous wildflowers you want to establish.

Initial considerations: Does the site contain any subsurface or surface archaeological features?

Are there any scarce annual wildflowers associated with arable fields present? These can often be present in the seed bank, and sometimes most abundant in field margins.

Is the site under drained? Are there drains around the field edge?

Early interventions: Block or remove any boundary and subsurface drainage.

Create scattered brash piles.

Excavate shallow pools of varying depths and create mounds and friable cliff faces with the arisings.

Scrape off the topsoil in some areas to reveal the chalk subsoil below. Create networks of banks with the arisings.

Locate nearby old chalk grassland sites. Get permission to collect seeds or hay from them.

Identify several areas of a few square metres to focus the introduction of wildflower seed.

Prepare a fine seedbed across these areas to be inoculated.

Brash harvest seed from species-rich donor sites in late summer. Broadcast the seed quickly; this can be done from around mid-August into September.

Plant up and fence scattered patches of native shrubs such as Dog Wood, Wayfaring Tree, Blackthorn and Field Rose.

Subsequent management: Facilitate very light, year-round, or occasional grazing by cattle free from anti-parasitic drugs.

Consider using a flail or volunteer group to very occasionally coppice areas of shrubs, in late January or February the aim being to maintain a mosaic of variable age shrub clamps. Doing this in late winter will give Wildlife time to consume all available seeds and berries.

Long-term development: In this example your aim is to maintain a species rich mosaic of open grassland with scattered shrubs. The brash piles and shrub clamps will, with any luck, draw in Rabbits. These will help to maintain shorter grazed lawns set within longer areas of flowering grassland.

In the short term, the herbaceous vegetation will be dominated by commoner wildflowers. But, given time, usually a few decades, scarcer wildflowers characteristic of older chalk grassland should begin to appear.

3.2 Improved pasture and amenity grassland

Context: Much of the lowland agricultural grassland we see on UK farmland would have been rich in wildflowers if it was grassland prior to the advent of chemical fertilisers. Many have been ploughed and re-seeded, fertilised and managed such that flowering plants are now few if present at all.

This loss of species-rich grassland is a major cause of farmland biodiversity loss. Creating a species-rich grassy shrubland on existing improved pasture is a great way to help nature recover on farmland.

Managed amenity grassland in towns and villages is generally rather bleak as far as wildlife is concerned but will likely have escaped heavy fertiliser inputs.

Re-establishing wildflowers within improved grassland can be challenging. The thick sward of grasses will be a difficult place for wildflowers to establish themselves compared to bare arable. You'll need to introduce a bit of sward disturbance to provide spots where the seeds can easily find contact with soil and germinate free from too much competition from the grasses.

Initial considerations: Select a species-poor site that's not too fertile and has an open, sunny aspect.

Early interventions: If the grasses are vigorous and the site fertile, harvest several unfertilised hay crops, at least once and ideally several times, during the initial couple of summers. Crucially, remove cut hay off site: don't allow cut material to decay on site as this simply returns nutrients to the soil. You're aiming to strip excess fertility and thereby favour wildflowers over more competitive agricultural grasses.

Consider reversing the effects of any sub-surface under-drainage and field edge drains.

Create brash piles scattered widely across the site.

Plant islands of native shrubs with a few trees, within fenced exclosures.

Consider scraping off areas of topsoil to reveal less fertile sub-soil, as long as there aren't archaeological remains that might be damaged.

Excavate scattered clean water pools; these should be a mix of seasonally and permanently wet.

Select a few 3-4m square areas where you'll introduce wildflowers. Strip these of grass and lightly cultivate to form a fine seed bed. Broadcast locally collected seed and spread green hay in late summer-early autumn. Wildflowers in these inoculated patches will gradually colonise more widely. If time and resources allow, enlarge the areas to be seeded as much as possible. If soil conditions are right, try to get and broadcast fresh Yellow Rattle seed. This species is parasitic on grasses and helps to reduce their vigour and competitive ability. This will favour wildflowers.

Consider setting up a small wildflower nursery at which you can grow small plugs of appropriate wildflower species for subsequent planting. Planting plugs in autumn can be a highly effective, if very labour intensive, way to get wildflowers established within permanent grassland.

Create small (a few square metre), lightly cultivated plots. Re-cultivate one or two annually, returning to cultivate a given plot every 1-3 years and longer for some. Maintain these as small plots of disturbance in the long-term.

Subsequent management: Lightly graze the site with cattle free from antiparasitic chemicals.

If possible, continue to import and spread green hay in mid to late July each year for, say, 3 to 4 years after initial establishment.

Continue to cultivate small plots on a varied rotation.

Long-term development: If you want your shrubland to remain open for sun-loving wildlife and grazing animals, ensure summer grazing pressure is very low. Invertebrates will benefit from chemical-free livestock dung in summer but you need to ensure that wildflowers can bloom and set seed profusely. With light cattle grazing, but no specific management of shrubby areas, the site would probably develop as enormously valuable wood pasture over a few decades.

3.3 Woodlands edge

Context: In this example we're aiming to maximise the potential for early successional woodland-associated species in a woodland expansion project. Here, we'll aim to optimise the early years for open habitat specialists while still delivering the longer-term objective of creating closed-canopy woodland, coppice, or more open wood pasture. We'll expand and link up two blocks of woodland separated by an open field of improved pasture or arable.

Rather than plant densely with whips, we'll facilitate the development of a more open, early successional grassland-shrubland habitat mosaic that will persist for, say, the first decade before closing up and moving towards woodland.

Also, an attempt is made to create conditions that might enable colonisation, all-be-it temporarily, by 'woodland' butterflies already present here.

Small, mixed-species groups of a few native tree and shrub seedlings are established using seedlings and seeds collected locally as well as, but in preference to, imported whips.

Within and around the edges of these shrub clumps, early action is taken to introduce native woodland edge flowering plant species, including the food plants of woodland specialist butterflies.

The open, sunny but sheltered conditions may draw them in from nearby woodland rides and glades. The caterpillar food plants you can consider introducing can be determined once you know which species are present in adjacent or nearby woodland and what they require. Butterfly Conservation provides guidance on food plants on its website.

Initial considerations: Ideally, select a strip along the sunny edge of the woodland block. Don't worry too much about deer density: they sculpt rather than scupper shrubland development.

Early interventions: Reverse any under-drainage and side drainage. Many lowland woodlands have been drained in the past, with surface ditches a common feature. This practice has dried out many of our woodlands relative to natural conditions. This may well have contributed to the decline of some woodland bird species.

Existing woodland should be rewetted, and newly created woodlands be set up to ensure a more natural hydrology.

Excavate a series of clean water pools and hollows. These will be sunny in the first decade or two and become increasingly shady through time. The wildlife communities using them will change accordingly.

Create widely scattered brash piles.

Plant groups of native trees and shrubs. Fence these if needed to exclude browsing animals. Consider using wattles or hurdles if they're available from nearby coppicing. Plant appropriate butterfly and moth caterpillar food plants within and at the edges of these clumps.

Subsequent management: Of course, one could manage this woodland edge Shrike Shrubland as a permanent open coppice-like mosaic if an aim is to maintain habitat for associated butterflies. Or it could be nudged towards open wood pasture with appropriate cattle grazing.

Alternatively, you can stand back and allow natural succession to proceed towards closed-canopy woodland.

Long-term development: With this example, the long-term aim is to enlarge and reconnect an area of woodland. Therefore, the site would be allowed to develop into close canopy woodland, coppice, or more open wood pasture. If close canopy woodland was the intention, one could acquire further land on its outer edge to create another block of shrubland, thereby gradually expanding the woodland outwards through time.

If, on the other hand, the intention is to maintain the area as more open habitat for woodland interior butterflies, a coppicing regime could be investigated. The exact prescription for this will depend on local circumstances.

4. Managing Shrike Shrublands

We've briefly considered longer term management in the immediately preceding sections. To recap, in your mind's eye, how would you like your shrubland to look in, say, 30 years? Are you aiming to develop woodland or wood pasture, or would you like to maintain it as an early-successional grassland shrubland mosaic?

If you're aiming at kicking-off the development of closed-canopy woodland, you can stand back after a few years having done the early groundwork described in previous chapters.

The site will move through its shrubland phase to a more closed thicket woodland stage. Trees and shrubs will colonise open areas from the planted islands and adjacent woodland and, after a few decades, you'll have a young, structurally-complex, biodiverse native woodland that'll accumulate an ever changing community of wildlife through time.

To achieve this, you'll need to be careful with the level of cattle grazing, a feature of management that is important for younger shrublands.

British woodlands once had herds of Aurochs (wild cattle) living within and moving through them, but much of the country was woodland, shrubland and wood pasture back then and these wild herds were free to move unimpeded across vast regions rather than being confined to small areas.

I cannot stress enough how important it is to ensure that cattle entering the shrubland are free from toxic antiparasitic chemicals. Dung is a hugely important habitat for a wide variety of invertebrates. Red-backed Shrikes may struggle to raise a brood in a shrubland without dung-associated beetles.

If rather than closed-canopy woodland, you're aiming to develop wood pasture, with, ultimately, scattered 'veteran' trees set with a shrubby 'parkland' with flower-rich, grazed lawns, you can afford slightly heavier grazing and browsing. It's not possible to prescribe stocking rates. They should be determined on a site-by-site basis and will probably require a degree of experimentation.

Any existing woodlands adjacent to your shrubland will very likely support both native and non-native deer. I don't consider even relatively high densities of deer to be as big a problem as others claim, but adding cattle *could* result in cumulative grazing and browsing pressure that's too high for woodland development. You'll have to use your judgement when deciding what if any browsing livestock to allow to enter the site in the longer term.

If you'd like to maintain the site as an open, early successional grassland-shrubland mosaic longer-term, you might combine cattle grazing and browsing with occasional volunteer 'scrub bashing' weekends or mechanical interventions to knock-back shrubby areas on a long rotational basis. Cut a different shrub mound during each operation, cutting each on, say, a ten-year rotation.

This sort of intervention may sound dramatic and destructive. But we once had Aurochs, Rhinos and Elephants crashing through UK shrublands. You're merely replicating ecosystem engineering and processes lost because humans drove European species of megafauna to extinction. Do this in late winter only.

Wild Boar is a key species and should be welcomed across its native range in the UK. Sadly, it's essentially ecologically extinct in the British countryside. Its rooting behaviour certainly looks dramatic and could be said to damage some anthropogenic habitats such as closed-sward, species-rich grassland. But, if present, the disturbance it generates should be welcomed within new shrublands.

Rabbits, although not native, create modest levels of ground disturbance that many plants and invertebrates depend on. The closely grazed lawns they create are used by many birds - not least Red-backed Shrikes - for hunting. Rabbits should be welcomed. Moles are another neglected native species whose hills provide little patches of disturbance that should be welcomed.

5. Discussion and conclusions

Hopefully this short book has inspired you to create, or encourage the creation of, Shrike Shrublands.

We could be creating hundreds of hectares of shrublands annually if only we slightly modified our approach to native woodland creation.

But species-rich shrublands deserve to be created in their own right, in addition to in areas intended for woodland creation. That's because mosaics of flowering grassland with scattered shrubs support a huge array of wildlife, including many species of conservation concern and priority.

What's more, grassy shrublands can provide excellent conditions for grazing livestock. This habitat is entirely compatible with wildlife friendly farming.

Hopefully, organisations engaged in the creation of new woodlands will more often than not adopt the shrubland approach set out here.

In a decade or so, if we have a shifting mosaic of emergent shrublands across the British countryside, we might just see the welcome return of the Butcher Bird to its rightful home in the British countryside.

6. Further reading

I'll provide a list of books and reports to read at my website: stevecjones.uk[1]

The JNCC scrub report can be downloaded here: https://hub.jncc.gov.uk/assets/39590874-8927-4c42-b02a-374712caccd6

---

1. http://stevecjones.uk

7. Acknowledgements

Thanks to the Knepp Estate, RSPB and Natural England for the opportunity to investigate the natural history of the Red-backed Shrike and for inspiring this booklet. The Knepp Estate is superb: emulating their efforts more widely, as part of one's farming system or in one's efforts to pursue rewilding and woodland creation through assisted natural regeneration, could be just what Shrikes need to stage a comeback.

8. About the author

Steve Jones has worked in UK and international wildlife conservation for nearly three decades. He can usually be found on the Isle of Wight, or Cornwall, in the northern summer, and somewhere close to the equator once the first frosts form on his van windscreen.

Find out more at his website: stevecjones.uk

If you enjoyed reading this booklet please consider leaving a review on your favourite online retail store website. This helps other people find it. Thank you.

Also by Steve Jones

Shrike Shrublands
Wildlife Watching Around Ventnor, Isle of Wight
Writers in the Wild

Watch for more at Stevecjones.uk.

About the Author

Steve has lived in Ventnor on the Isle of Wight on and off since 1995. An avid 'patch watcher', Steve considers Ventnor to be by far the best bird watching patch he's ever had. He's keen to encourage other bird watchers and naturalists to explore the area.

Read more at Stevecjones.uk.